ANCHOR BOOKS

POETIC WORDS FROM LONDON & HOME COUNTIES

Edited by

Heather Killingray

First published in Great Britain in 1997 by
ANCHOR BOOKS
1-2 Wainman Road, Woodston,
Peterborough, PE2 7BU
Telephone (01733) 230761

All Rights Reserved

Copyright Contributors 1997

HB ISBN 1 85930 478 8
SB ISBN 1 85930 473 7

FOREWORD

Anchor Books is a small press, established in 1992, with the aim of promoting readable poetry to as wide an audience as possible.

We hope to establish an outlet for writers of poetry who may have struggled to see their work in print.

The poems presented here have been selected from many entries. Editing proved to be a difficult task and as the Editor, the final selection was mine.

Poetic Words From London And The Home Counties is a fine collection of poetry, which has been contributed from poets from this particular area.

The poets delve deep into their emotions to express through their poetic words how they feel about everyday issues which concern them. The poems reflect their opinions on today's society, the style and theme is varied throughout the anthology.

Most of all poets are united in their passion for poetry, and I trust will be a riveting read by young and old alike, and will leave you delighted by its content for years to come.

I trust this selection will delight and please the authors and all those who enjoy reading poetry.

Heather Killingray
Editor

CONTENTS

The Waiting Game	Janet Hodgson	1
Candle Flame	Rosemary Drewett	2
Home Girl, Mirabelle	Margaret Andrews	3
Forbidden Love	Mo Dawson	4
Afternoon Tea	Olivia Erskine	5
A Decade Of Drowning	Daniel Vickery	6
Prettiest Skull	Robert Hammond	7
Love, The Deceiver	Neil Innes	8
For Special Grandparents	Diane Cooper	9
Rocking Horse	C Leith	10
New Woman	Sue Gutteridge	11
How Can I Tell You?	Paula Hind	12
Madness	Cathie Fleming	13
Winging Thoughts	Ruth Daviat	14
Fishing In The River Lea	Albert Moses	15
Tree Lover	Joan Heybourn	17
A Rambler	P B Sewell	18
My Nan	Jo Lee	19
Redundancy	John Thorpe	20
The Whale	Emma Heatley	21
The Magic Stocking	Andrew Deans	22
A Winter Scene	M Lucke	23
A Gas Connection	Maggie Grierson	24
Fast Decay	Paul Hetherington	25
Enigma Of A Rose	Joyce Dobson	26
A Present	Vanessa Miles	28
Whispers Of Deceit	Anthony George Querino	30
The Day The Earth Stood Still	William Flood	31
My Cat	Carole Kaye	32
Life	Melvyn Roiter	33

A Lasting Christmas	J J Murray	34
The Worm Slithered	Dave Julian	35
Couth Potato	Hope Ash	36
Putney Bridge	Winifred Curran	37
Where Endings Must	James Parry	38
In The Midst Of London	John Christopher Cole	39
The Bluebells	Diane Campbell	40
Narcissus	Philip Eley	41
The Tenant	Mary O'Hara	42
Paradise	Zoe Fisher	43
I Want It To Be Morning	Gavin Hodgson	44
Fox In The Rain	Leah Carpenter	45
Loving You	Phyllis R Harvey	46
Life	J Pearson	47
Sonnet To A Lady	Graham O'Connor	48
A Moment In Time	Diana Meek	49
Easter - What Is It?	Julita McIntosh	50
Cinema	Chas Warlow	51
Help	Oliver Cox	52
Dawning Sea	Zoe Ryle	53
Dal Lake	Rachael Noronha	54
Essence	Laura Annansingh	55
Rejection	NAT	56
Faithful Friend	Colin Taylor	57
The Mobile Phone	Ron Duck	58
Spancil My Thoughts For They May Spancil Me	Margaret Dunne	59
The Demise Of Big - Bad 'Butcher-Ben'	Xerox (Psyche) Pendragon	60
The Storm	Julieanne Jude Murphy	62
Rain	Alasdair Aston	63
I Am No Longer	Natasha Cameron	64
Jobber's Blues	John A Singh	65
The Bride	Eunice Patel	66
Shopping	Catherine Isichei	67

The Boy	J Davies	68
The Duel	James Poole	69
Untitled	P Schofield	70
Only A Street Away	Jean Beith	71
Hope	Wendy Edwards	72
London Traffic Jam	P S Joll	73
The Land	Valerie Deering	74
Udderly Cowed	Bryn Bartlett	75
You've Come Out To Play	Emma Lawrence	76
Taraf	Linda Miller	77

THE WAITING GAME

The hours you wait
before a date,
are often very dull.
It's raining out, you've nothing to do.
You've washed your hair and brushed your shoes
You sit and watch the clock hands move,
until you've applied and removed
you make-up three times or more.
How you long for that knock on the door.

What time is it?
It's five past eight!
You could murder that boy, he's always late
ten past now, and still no word.
Wait a minute, what's that you heard,
A knock, you rush downstairs.
Now he's come, you have no cares.
Bye mum and dad, see you soon,
and gone is that dreary afternoon.

Janet Hodgson

CANDLE FLAME

So dark the night
Inside my soul
So bright the candle flame
That made me whole.

So strong the ties that bind
Unravel me
These cords, this love
That cannot be.

And yet the candle flame
Burns brightly still
Times I cannot forget
And fear I will.

To huddle near the flame
To cling to times long past
This is my foolishness, my hope
To make it last.

Light up the candle flame
Once more -
I need to feel its glow
The love I cannot name
The love I want to know.

Rosemary Drewett

HOME GIRL, MIRABELLE

Strange, the things which Mirabelle scrawls across the page,
Smiling faces, noseless in some cases, an occasional scowl and indignant rage!
'Was I as talented an artist at her age?' I enquire of mother;
I had not underestimated her, but neither expected so much of her.
Strange, the things which Mirabelle sometimes in glee utter,
Stranger still the language which she has picked up from the *gutter* -
I certainly would not have used such language for mother to hear,
I could not have ranted, raged so much or even swear.

Mirabelle added a new dimension to our young married lives,
Simon and I often *had to* accept her bribes,
When we were busy she often had her own way,
Hoodwinked us into allowing her friends to stay and play.
Were we such rebels at her tender age, wisened and worldly wise aged seven years -
And gave massive headaches to our parents, the poor old dears?
I suppose we must have given them cause for concern -
But everyday we observe her behaviour and from her quite a lot we learn.

What will she be like in her teenage years?
We anticipate the worse always, have so many fears.
Will she be rebellious, a terror running wild -
Or will she be our pearl, a devoted and dutiful *child?*
Strange, how we panic when she arrives home later than agreed -
Our house rules are not so strict - nothing to which she could not heed;
And stranger still the friends which she now invites home for us to meet -
But we are overjoyed when they are gone and she nests at our feet.

Margaret Andrews

FORBIDDEN LOVE

I watch you in the sunlight and see the contours of your face
My heart is so sure now . . . no-one could take your place
Your smile so ever ready and your touch is sure and strong
How can we feel faint hearted . . . how can this love be wrong?
Do you think you will always love me
Do you think you will always care
Whenever I'm sad and lonely, please say that you'll be there
Yes my heart skips a beat when I see you
I'm so glad for the sound of your voice
I wonder why you chose to love me . . .
When of so many you have the choice
Are you sure you will love me forever
And hold me within your heart
To honour, love and cherish, never, oh never to part
Please say you will be my lovely, my lover, my partner in life
To watch over one another, though never to be your wife.

Mo Dawson

AFTERNOON TEA

They sit in wicker bedroom chairs
A motley collection on the lawn
Faded images of their former selves
Idling away the remnants of their lives
The old stone wall shades their parchment skin
Gay parasol lends unbidden festive air

Retired colonel, moustache a-bristling, eyes a-twinkling
His muttered words unheard by the unhearing
Maiden lady, bedecked in straw hat
Skirt pulled firmly over close-pressed knees
Little finger crooked to raise China tea
In porcelain cup to pallid lips
Old Maud, beaming a smile at one and all
Is happy - just being!
Daisy, with unseeing eyes, exists in her own personal world
Happy or sad? Who can tell? For she utters never a word
Accepting plastic cup, she drinks when bidden
Violet knits on and on, dropping stitch after stitch in haste
So proud of her creation
What love is worked into that *lacy* dishcloth!

The endless summer afternoon is whiled away in dreams
As drowsily they feed on oft-remembered times
I feel an intruder in their private world
And creep softly away, unseen and unheard
Wondering if one day I'll be called to join their ranks!

Olivia Erskine

A DECADE OF DROWNING

*'For so long my unconscious has pursued me like a charade,
a restless soul creating the future and past.'*

Locked in a dream unable to wake,
reality disappears and fiction overtakes

Someone help push me to the surface,
I am drowning under this turbulence

Nature watching comforts slip away,
memories fade to a patchwork shade of grey

Limp skin layers my hands,
unable to reach anything so far away from friends

Sea water splashes side to side inside,
lungs nearly full, a few drops to overkill

A watery grave summoning me in,
the falling current is only helping

Where is the exit, never brought my ticket,
looking for the end only to see another life begin

Is this freedom of fear in dream,
subsidence again,
reality proceeded this course

so fiction is the conscious source . . .

Daniel Vickery

PRETTIEST SKULL

Among her scraps of life, deep coral,
Under the surface of paste stones and sweet powder
And over too many letters never sent,
One conversation too many holds high
A pretence, her last great deception.
Scraps of stone,
Textured, structured like pieces of bone
Beneath my feet,
Fragments of sweetness,
In your beautiful cranium,
Your prettiest skull.

Among the words she bled,
Perfectly read, forming hand to head things
Cutting away to the light,
The last thing I wanted to say unsaid,
Dead in the water, holding me under.
Past - the way that mouth could be,
Loving and killing, all over me,
Heart pulling, gravitating, burning me.

I saved you a piece of summer,
Black grease chain palm,
Dirt, greens, stones and everything,
Anything to feel some love again.

You were textured, structured through pieces of bone,
Your prettiest skull over fragments of stone.

Robert Hammond

LOVE, THE DECEIVER

Love, I never called on you,
You knocked upon my door;
And so beguiled me with your kiss,
That I just yearned the more.
You spoke to me of happiness:
Of ecstasy and joy.
Little did I realise,
I would become your toy.

Love, you bade me chance my all:
In a gambler's desperate bid.
Now the loser,
I must fall.
Yet you think of me a fool;
Your mocking chant I still recall:
'Far better to have loved and lost,
Than never loved at all.'

Love, you whisper oh so softly;
Sweet and honeyed is your call;
But yours is far the bitterest pill:
Far bitter yet than gall.

Oh love, is there to be no last embrace;
No final fond adieu?
You could at least just grant me that.
I gave my all to you.
Alas, you are a creature of the night;
That with the breaking of the dawn,
Must hide your face and take your flight.

Neil Innes

FOR SPECIAL GRANDPARENTS

When we open the book of memories
We will find you there
though death has parted us, we are bound in love
Keep me alive by sharing those times we had together
Smile for me, for I am at peace
don't be afraid to mention my name
speak my words, my sayings, my phrases
Use my knock at the door
for you are in reaching distance
Only a thought away
your presence a whisper on the wind
your smile will brighten our days
and the memories we treasure
will last a lifetime.

Diane Cooper

ROCKING HORSE
(For the children of Dunblane)

The rocking horse stands silent, no toys on the floor.
Your dolls are all packed away, a sweet memory from a time before.
A photograph to remember you, an innocent little face,
a video to hear your laughter and the sound your voice used to make.

Your rocking horse stands silent now,
no creaking upon the floorboards,
sitting there to remember, of a time we were happy once before.

We still miss you, even after all this time,
taken away from us, by a crime against mankind.

The house seems colder now, no longer a home will it be,
just two lonely people, where once a shell used to be.

The rocking horse plays no more, pinning for that little girl,
who played with him for ever more . . .

C Leith

NEW WOMAN

Stop body stop, no more to indulge,
Be assertive battle that bulge.
Get the mind in gear be alert to win,
Pop off now enrol in the local gym.
Loads of press-ups then onto the bike,
Let my mind wander think what I like.
Trendy in my leotard hair neatly in a plait,
Suddenly vulnerable, and extremely fat.
Park myself upon this enormous rowing machine,
Half and hour on this one come off feeling lean.
Sunday a bit of jogging down a country lane,
All of this exercise life will never be the same.
Thursday night is swimming I promise no more chips,
Only fizzy spring water and just take dainty sips.
I'll give it a month if I have not lost a stone,
I shall get a bag of crisps watch TV and stay at home.

Sue Gutteridge

HOW CAN I TELL YOU?

How can I tell you of raging fear,
Felt in my heart when I feel you near,
Of how I can't reach you, and why I don't try,
And ill-gotten memories which lead me to cry.

How can I tell you of what you've done,
The way you've changed this innocent one,
Taken the love and left the pain,
Afraid of being alone again.

How can I tell you I want you to stay,
To care and to hold me and not go away,
Need all your warmth and your loving desire,
To chase insecurities into the fire.

How can I tell you that this is the last,
The make or break of a wretched past,
My fears of the future and how they taunt me,
Wake me at night and continually haunt me.

How can I tell you what leaving would do,
How I'd never recover from loving you,
That although I'm addicted I'm scared to care,
Afraid that tomorrow you won't be there.

How can I tell you all this?

Paula Hind

MADNESS

He hurts
The pain is suffocating
The emptiness, infinite
The future, non-existent
The questioning, destructive

She watches
The scene is torturous
The desire to reach out, unbearable
The rejection, frustrating
Her being, invisible

You
I
Searching
Trudging
Questioning

Missing the point.

Cathie Fleming

WINGING THOUGHTS

An ex Fleet Air Arm writer wren,
I watch the matelots march erect
In peacetime yet I see again
The havoc of war in retrospect.

Comrades I strode with side by side
And the proud, dignified salute,
The planes I saw, archangels, glide,
Part of a pattern in grim dispute.

Confidential cog in a wheel
An infinitesimal pawn of war
Yet there's nostalgia still I feel
Some decades after the battle roar.

Conflict disrupted phase of youth
But I'm hearing laughter strung with tears,
Those innocents, mainstay of truth,
Tools of the bombing, hiding our tears.

I question was it really I,
Was I that actress on drama stage,
Pretending joy when up in the sky
Our heroes soared in that bygone age?

That chapter - is it ever closed,
The aura of unreality,
Discomforts that those times imposed,
Doubt as to what our futures might be?

Sometimes when I walk late at night,
Bejewelled, an aircraft sails above,
I watch, thrilled, till it sails from sight,
A buddy I acknowledge with love.

Ruth Daviat

FISHING IN THE RIVER LEA

I sit by the river Lea,
as it runs for ever free

I see a youngster fishing rod in hand,
sitting comfortably on the bank

He is going about it by the book,
will he ever get a fish on the hook?

The sun is high in the sky,
and time goes so slowly by.

The boy feels just fine,
as he sits watching his line.

A seagull has come to watch him fish,
it is thinking of a good dish

It makes a squawking noise,
with a rather interesting poise.

The line moves fast signalling a bite,
the boy pulls but didn't do it right

The fish happily swims away,
but may be caught another day

The boy is roaring with laughter,
after all he could catch it later

The boy smiles at his lost chance,
and strangely does a peculiar dance.

His dog comes back after a walk,
sits next to him as if to talk

'Come home' the dog must have said,
he started packing, that's what he did

As they walked past me back home,
silhouetted by the church dome

I could see the sun going down,
not to be seen until the dawn.

Albert Moses

TREE LOVER

Oh, give me the woodlands, oh, give me a tree,
What else holds such beauty and rapture for me?
Oh give me their coolness, their peace and their shade,
Within a cathedral of leaf, branch and glade.

Oh give me the woodlands, the crackle of leaves
'Neath my feet in the autumn, wonderland weaves
Colours of russet, brown, gold, amber and red,
With evergreens towering high overhead.

Oh give me the woodlands with pine trees so tall
When frosty icicles encircle them all,
A fairyland wonder of glistening white
As soft snowy flakes settle during the night.

Oh give me the woodlands as spring comes anew
When green grassy glades are bespeckled with dew,
The soft leaves all whispering secrets above
Whilst trembling anew at the coo of the dove.

For of all the rare beauty found on this earth
There's non so enduring with grandeur and worth
As forest and woodlands with their rustling leaves,
Oh give me my beautiful picture of trees.

Joan Heybourn

A RAMBLER

As I ramble through the pass
Between the mountains high
I sometimes sit upon the grass
And gaze up in the sky
I look for the Golden Eagle
A very splendid bird
And if it's quiet, I will hear its call
Like no other I have heard.
Soon it's time, to be on my way once more
Passing primroses, bluebells, by the score
Slowly walking down the hill
Beside a stream that's never still
Passing falls and a little bridge
Ragged sheep upon the ridge
A deer or two, maybe a hare
Mischievous squirrels playing there.
Now I've reached the road below
Left the mountains, their peaks in snow
The countryside is rough and crude
This lovely Cumbria in solitude.

P B Sewell

MY NAN

I used to sit in my nan's room
She used to tell me stories
About bombs going boom.
I used to sit on her bed
Looking and listening
To every word she said.

Nan used to make them funny
We used to laugh
It made my life so sunny
I can remember playing cards
On my birthday in September
I was only nine!

Then we had to move away
Nan said 'Don't worry, things are going to be just fine,
You'll see. And there's always another day.'
The sadess day of my life
Is when we drove away from my only home
It felt like someone stabbed me with a knife

I visited my nan once a week
They were the days I remember the most.
But then nan died
All my memories came
Flooding back.

I just laid on my bed
Thinking and crying
I never thought the day would come
It hit me like nothing else before
And I will never forget her
Because she was *my nan.*

Jo Lee

REDUNDANCY

We never choose to do a thing until it's far too late,
We have to get our diary out to check the time and date.
It's 'hurry here' and 'hurry there' throughout the blesséd day
With shouts to one another 'Are you free on Saturday?'

I can't wait 'til I am sixty when retirement day is due,
But suddenly what's this I hear - it comes right out the blue.
I must start clearing out my desk - that really is a shock,
Redundancy has come at last and now I must take stock.

I sit here thinking of those days when things were always rushed
And wish those days were here again and not just in the past.
The moral of this story is just thank your lucky stars
That you have even got a job while others out there starve.

John Thorpe

THE WHALE

He lay there cold as ice
As sad as crying sea lion.
His eyes looked hard as he stared out to sea, longing
to be free.
People came around laughing like hyenas in the
echoing rocks.
I stood there looking at the slick skin shining like
silk.
He groaned and slashed his tail like a hurtling
tornado crashing down, the sand rose up like a puff
of smoke.
People came running from here and there and
they started pushing the *whale* out to sea. He
groaned in fear and
I just stood there looking at him with pity.
As he came near the sea he rolled gracefully like
the Mary Rose as it sank into the cold black ocean.

Emma Heatley (12)

THE MAGIC STOCKING

I will put in the stocking
the scrumptious smell of roast turkey with tasty
stuffing,
the softness of a cuddly brown teddy,
the bounce of a fluffy pink rabbit.

I will put in the stocking
the whooshing flight of a brightly coloured
toy plane,
the shininess of Ruldolph's red nose,
the sparkle of a bright new star.

I will put in the stocking
the delicious taste of a smooth milk chocolate
button,
the crunchiness of icy, white snow,
the beautiful pattern of dancing snowflakes.

My stocking is fashioned from round snowballs,
the sparkle of icicles hanging like sharp teeth and
patches of red the colour of Santa's cloak.

In my stocking I will build an enormous snowman
with a lump of black coal for his eyes and an
orange carrot for his nose.

Andrew Deans

A WINTER SCENE

I look out on the frosty scene.
The grass is white instead of green.
I'd like to go for a long walk
But that of course is idle talk.

I'm old - my bones would likely break
Not one step can I safely take,
My feet just slip upon the ice
And down I fall in just a trice.

Won't some young man come - hold my arm,
I'd turn on all my old, old, charm.
If we both fell down together
I'd forget the bad, bad, weather.

M Lucke

A GAS CONNECTION

It was on a Friday morning the gas man came to call;
'Good morning, do come in' I said, as he stepped into the hall.
'I am quite ready for you; have put newspapers on the floor.
The poor man looked so perplexed; on his face a frown he wore.
'Ready? Ready for what?' he asked;
'To read the meter is my task.'
Then it became clear he had taken fright;
He became agitated and turned very white.
With great haste the meter was read;
Before I could thank him he had fled.
As arranged the engineer arrived 'tho late;
To him my tale I did relate.
'It's his body he thought you were after'
He said, creasing up with raucous laughter.
Now I think I should just mention,
Nothing untoward was my intention.
So be careful when a gas man's expected;
Make sure with which Department he's connected.

Maggie Grierson

FAST DECAY

A sperm, an egg, a union,
Life for all begins the same,
You start as a single cell,
Simplest living creature known,
Fast multiplication, division and differentiation.

Tiny naked creature,
Learning fast, soon to speak,
Growing up, wearing clothes,
Going to school and learning,
Fast multiplication, division and differentiation.

Take examinations, leave school,
Going to university and socialising,
Making plans for the future,
Set yourself up in business,
Fast multiplication, division and differentiation.

Now you are a prosperous executive,
Ignoring the pleas of your workers,
Hating freedom and socialism,
Finally a trade union forms,
Fast multiplication, division and differentiation.

The workers seize power,
Your bourgeoisie principals toppled,
The people's country at last,
You perish as an equal,
Fast multiplication, division and differentiation.

The unicellular bacteria triumph,
The great puromycin revolution,
You go the way of all the people,
Consumed by the simplest forms,
Slow division, multiplication and integration.

Paul Hetherington

ENIGMA OF A ROSE
(For Rose FE!)

When her peers do nothing but dust and cook,
The Rose adds a line to her 'little black book!'

Faded? - A little. Perhaps past her prime?
No! For she has the means to slow down time.

Disguising herself in clothes, somewhat grey,
The Rose - she waits - for that special day.

Hugging her secret, close to her chest -
She pities her peers, and most of the rest.

This Rose - she refuses to fade and to die,
And to leave behind, only, a soft velvet sigh.

She bubbles over, with a vain selfish glee -
And waits for the burgeon of illicit ecstasy!

Each bitter-sweet union; each tender letter;
Heralds fresh meetings - the longer - the better.

The Rose in her prime: with knowledge of life -
Having been daughter; lover; mother and wife.

This lover - un-named - is lucky, for sure -
This Rose - ever eager - to open the door,

To a heaven on earth; the butterfly hour;
That builds - or destroys - such is its power!

This Rose needs the love; the affection; the act;
That's not flight of fancy - it's a cold and hard fact!

Without it, the Rose, would wither and die -
If it weren't for the man - that takes her so high.

The Rose fears, not all, her actions condone,
'Too bad!' is the mutter of a Rose that's full-blown.

Her peers yearly age, aware with great pain,
Inevitably - each Summer - the Rose - blooms again!

Joyce Dobson

A PRESENT

My son gives me flowers
I ask why.
He looks at me, smiles,
'No reason,' he replies
and in that moment
he is the man, I the child.

Vanessa Miles

WHISPERS OF DECEIT

There was no shortage
Of a lack of understanding
There was a guilty rhythm
To my suspicious heart

But all you seem to do is laugh

I won't crawl
Crawl on my knees back to you
I'll get by without you
I won't plead
Because your love
Is something I no longer need
But I still hold the guilt
It's something I still feel I need

Guilty rhythm
Whispers about you
Whispers about me
Whispers about the two of us
Don't you know people talk
Listen to them can't you fear
Can you hear their guilty lies
From their whispers of deceit

We don't talk all we do is fight
It was the wrong situation
For a sleepless night
That kept us awake with fight all night

No I'll never
Take a chance with someone else
The way you took chances with me
That's not how it's going to be
You've taken the rhythm from my life
And everything else from my heart
I should have guessed
I should have known right from the start

Guilty rhythm
Whispers about you
Whispers about me
Whispers about the two of us
Don't you know people talk
Listen to them can't you fear
Can you hear their guilty lies
From their whispers of deceit

Now if that's fine with you
Then it's fine with me
I couldn't care less anymore
Just take a long look
Then you would see

My guilty heart
Has long since gone

And the memory of you too
Will soon be
Gone . . .

Anthony George Querino

THE DAY THE EARTH STOOD STILL

Was there ever a time,
when the earth stood still,
everyone was there,
you can still feel the chill,
from every profession,
to every career,
no-one missed out,
on this hemisphere,
the day goes down,
in histories distorted facts,
we were all linked together,
with one single act,
people from all nations,
mothers with babies,
from political men,
to extravagant ladies,
everyone knows exactly,
they remember where they were,
I was only four,
and even I was there!,
will we ever forget,
don't believe the lies,
do you think we all survived,
the day Kennedy died!

William Flood

MY CAT
(A true story)

Hello pussy cat of mine,
Why ever do you moan and whine?
Did mummy put your breakfast out?
Why do you look at me with doubt?
Did I forget some task today?
I guess I did your wide eyes say.
Water, biscuits, something else?
I can't think what I must confess.
A little warmth, a stroke, a hug?
Why pounce on me and pull and tug?
Your amber eyes . . . they're telling me
Something I just cannot see.
Your slender tail is hanging down,
You droopy funny little clown.
Why don't you go outside today
To run and leap and stalk your prey?
Your cry is deep - I know not why,
'Tis not like you my little fry.
What's that I see, is it the moon?
My plants need water very soon.
I fill my jug and out I go.
Oh no! . . . The flap is locked, I didn't know.
Dear pussy cat, my feline friend,
Now surely do I comprehend.
You faithful cat, so clean, refined,
What a clever little mind.
You must have been in pain somewhat
Just because I had forgot.
When nature called you could not go -
Your door was locked. I didn't know.

Carole Kaye

LIFE

When baby's born
To gasp for air
The first with all its might
A rat race to grow up into
Its place, to have to fight
Drivers, dealers, artists, clerks
Tailor, sir or dame
Whichever we may be through life
The end we see the same.

Melvyn Roiter

A LASTING CHRISTMAS

Snowflakes falling all around,
All is quiet without a sound,
Chimney pots line the sky,
As Christmas Day passes by,
But Christmas is meant to last -
The year,
To give us peace,
And good cheer.

J J Murray

THE WORM SLITHERED

The worm slithered from out of the ground
All silken skinned and brown
Its fore paused as it struck the cold fresh air
Then all courage it came right out into the stark dawn
Like a miniature snake it wriggled along the earth
A fat pigeon eyed this big fat juicy gourmet meal with wanton desire
But giant me was there the protector of this alien subterranean creature
this being from a world beneath the ground
Where only darkness and damp are its habitat
It turned on its belly in revelry of joy at escaping its manacles of earth
But I decided all judge and jury that it would be safer underground
Perhaps in its mind it wanted freedom at the risk of life
But I dug a hole and like a warden returned it to its dark cell.

Dave Julian

COUCH POTATO

What is a couch potato?
Is it a potato sitting on a
Settee or is it a person
Watching TV every minute
Of the day,
No conversation, no movement,
Just staring at the TV screen
Each minute, of the day,
Lack of exercise, putting on
Weight, losing contact with
The outside world.
A couch potato is a person
Who sits all day.

Hope Ash

PUTNEY BRIDGE

I stopped in the middle of the bridge for a while,
Memories of Putney, to my face brought a smile,
Look on to the Thames, and think back to the days,
Of Oxford and Cambridge - the boat race in haze,
Sweet memories of Putney in days long ago,
My landscape has changed, for the better, I know,
Days in Westminster, all travel no play,
On buses and tubes, I spent most of my day,
I mixed with the jet-set, in Chelsea of course,
On the common at weekends I'd gallop my horse,
I stand on the bridge, just a tourist today,
So glad that I met you, you took me away,
The view is so different, I look over the scene,
My heart now in Kerry, views fit for a Queen.

Winifred Curran

WHERE ENDINGS MUST

I take a day to live a day,
Each hour used without consent
From one another's document . . .
And go I forward where death lay.

Supposen, am I lost in vain
Report of all things in the world
Where I have rested, fallen, curled
Into a foetal-ball insane.

The lasting senses rich with strife
That harries, beckons, passions flare
Amongst the bludgeoned blossom's glare . . .
I thrust eternal's blameless knife.

I'll sleep here 'til the morning come
With thoughts of fairer chore and trance;
Where can I cover my head's dance
Of horror, reeling, wise-and-numb?

Events go on where'er I die,
And lose their value in this age
That leaves its bloodied-mark a page
O'er page . . . until no matter by.

The end of earth - the darkness falls -
Yet somewhere 'jellied eel' may sway
In acid-mud to crawl as may,
Man did when his small planet stalls.

My mark forgot, its message dust,
And galaxies revealed to close;
The passages-of-merit rose,
Now fallen out . . . where endings must.

James Parry

IN THE MIDST OF LONDON

I was in the heart of London.
The traffic was passing noisily by.
The capital was going about its business.
The sun was beginning to sink lower.

It had been a glorious day
But now the evening cool was taking over.
Still the ice-cream salesman plied their trade,
For hot days were their very lifeblood
And while the sun still shone business was good.

This was London. Where ancient listed buildings
Stood beside the oneness of modern design.
This was London. Where the pace of life
Left each visitor feeling breathless.

Yet still just off the busy thoroughfares
Were treasured little patches of grassland,
Covered on days of sunshine with bodies
Lying shirtless with no regard for dignity,
Briefly escaping from their busy offices.

It was there in the desert's oasis
That I found a tiny uninhabited spot,
Sheltered by trees that had stood for years
And with saplings planted for future generations.
There there were. Standing erect and proud.
A wonderful spread of bluebells,
Each individually crafted by Nature's hand.

They had withstood the heat of the day.
Now they eagerly drank in the cooler air.
They just didn't seem to belong there.
As I sat beside them I felt their beauty
And silently I rejoiced.

John Christopher Cole

THE BLUEBELLS

The bluebells in the woods
Smell so very sweet.
The bluebells in the woods,
Be careful, not to tread under feet,
My mum would take me to see bluebells bloom.
Such happiness on hot and sunny days,
But now my life is full of gloom,
I miss the simple things we did,
I miss my mum so bad,
I love my dearest mum,
That's why I'm feeling sad,
One day, we'll meet again,
Together we will be,
To see the bluebells bloom with mum,
Would truly make me happy.

Diane Campbell

NARCISSUS

Carelessly we cross the bridge
We cross the bridge
Across the river
The river knows as I know
There is nothing I could give her.

Candidly she remarks
At how the flowers laugh at us
Love hits me at that moment like a shiver
Does the water in this fountain ever reach the river?

All these buildings which a thousand, thousand men and more
Have marvelled at.
All these trees and flowers
Could satisfy a poet for a thousand, thousand hours.
Yet still it's just a simple look from her which makes me shiver
Does the water in this fountain ever reach the river?

T S Elliott, Thomas Hardy and Jane Austen
Make strange bedfellows in her bag
All their starling words
And stunning prose
Falling around together
Whispering to each other
Making her arm heavy with their history,
Reminding me of a further mystery,
It's the way she knew about the flowers which makes me shiver
And does the water in this fountain ever reach the river?

Philip Eley

THE TENANT

He slipped from the house
before morning had even begun
to show the merest hint of light
- a ghost, noiseless
but for the scrape of a mouse
and made his way somewhere
though I don't know where.

If I was there
he'd grunt as he passed me,
always sulking,
no time for talking.
'I have work to do'
he would sometimes swear
and shuffle on his way,
leaving the whole day curious,
then startle us at cocoa
as he thumped the steps hard
to his dingy share.

And the only clue he left
to his occupation
was a smell of incense
and ash on every stair.

Mary O'Hara

PARADISE

'Here is paradise'
Someone wrote that, on a subway wall
For a joke
That's all
'I'd hate to see hell'
Wrote some other joker
And next to that:-
'Hell is being a non-smoker'
And so it goes on
Dodging damp patches, missing tiles
Glaring at cowering litter
Hard and bitter
To be whitewashed one day
Forgotten, in the name of cleanliness
And what that disillusioned pen had to say -
In its own way
Is gone as well
- To paradise? -
To hell.

Zoe Fisher

I WANT IT TO BE MORNING

I want it to be morning
I want it to be light
I want the day to take me
And give me back my sight
I want an end to darkness
This fear that if I slip
A black dog will attack me
And hold me in its grip
I want to pack a suitcase
Rush headlong north by rail
To meet a country parson
And beauty in a veil
I want a Lutyens river-house
All honeysuckled bricks
A skewbald horse, an orchard
A pool, a 356
The sound of children laughing
In summer's drowsy haze
I want the smell of new-mown grass
And never-ending days
I want to go exploring
With Sophie, Tom and Jane
To show them how to bivouac
And make a daisy-chain
I want to think up treasure-hunts
And hide the clues at dawn
I want to build a bonfire
To throw our worries on
I want to write these lines for hours
To shield me from the night
I want it to be morning
I want it to be light.

Gavin Hodgson

FOX IN THE RAIN

Early on Thursday evening,
Just a twilight fell,
Raindrops pitter-pattered on the ground
The roofs and trees as well.

There was magic in the air
The light was shimmering and brilliant.
A fox crept through a hole in the hedge
Looking like a drowned rat.

Every time the rain fell harder,
Hit rubbish and leaves and made a sound,
He stood still on the lawn,
Perked his ears and glanced around.

Again, the rain plunged violently:
Once more, he surveyed around
He hesitated for a moment
Unable to find the source of the sounds.

Turning tail, through the hole,
Again he crawled, not bothered at all.
Still he sniffed, on the other side,
And quickly nipped up the wall.

He hopped a protruding branch
And persevered with his trip.
He stopped and looked at the sky.
Into his eyes some rain dripped.

Without looking about again
He turned on his haunches and leapt
His bushy tail remained, twitching.
A second later, he descended, soaking wet.

Leah Carpenter

LOVING YOU

To you my dear, with eyes that shine
And tender heart that blends with mine
I offer my eternal love
As constant as the stars above.
Like early rose with morning dew
I'll spend my days caressing you
Could changing seasons e'er compare
With beauty of a love so fair?

Phyllis R Harvey

LIFE

Life is good, sometimes bad
The things that happen can
Make you feel sad
Sometimes the sky is grey or blue
Sometimes you just don't know what to do

But there are such good things in life
The animals, flowers and music
Our families and memories.

For just like the seasons come and go
The sun, rain and snow
Life has its ups and downs
But don't forget to go with the flow!

J Pearson

SONNET TO A LADY

How sweet the lips that I would die to kiss
and in that warm caress find bliss unbound.
To take your hand and then to tell you this,
in you, my own true love, at last, I've found.
How sweet your eyes, that like the star lights shine.
My wish, for your rich beauty has no peer;
is take you in my arms and make you mine
and until time does end, to hold you near.
How sweet my dreams, for there I see your face,
when fiery passions on our souls do feed
and lovers games we play in nights embrace
where Aphrodite's song is all we heed.
So come with me and make this dream come true
and I will spend my life in loving you.

Graham O'Connor

A MOMENT IN TIME

Life is but a moment
That slips through your hands
And for the brief time you have it
It makes many demands
You struggle from day to day
Living life in the best possible way
Till that moment has passed
Passed you by all too fast
Now we have done our best
We can now lay down and rest.

Diana Meek

EASTER - WHAT IS IT?

Where has the feeling of Easter gone?
When everyone would dress up
When a trip to church was on
Then we'd eat our eggs and drinks we'd sup

I remember when I was younger
And the whole preparation of Easter-Lent
Was a very important time
I'd really take it serious, I knew what it meant

Lent was a time of self-sacrifice
It wasn't just giving up food
It had a spiritual meaning
But now with the media hype it's crude

I can't understand why people insist
That we teach children about yesteryear
When we the adults have long since forgot
The real meaning of Easter, how can kids fare?

Are we really being honest?
Saying that Jesus died for us
When all we seem to do right now
Is sit in judgement of each other, that's sus'

But getting back to Easter
A festival I really enjoy
Yes, I like the eggs and chicks
But to shop-owners it's all a ploy!

Julita McIntosh

CINEMA

See your dream
Up on the screen
There's a movie showing tonight
Everyone's cherished illusions
Up on the screen tonight
Doesn't matter if you're rich or poor
(So long as you've got the right amount)
Don't matter if you're black or white
You're gonna make it big tonight.

See that gleam at the back of the stalls?
That's the light of our fascination,
Flickering lantern, showing
Cool repose on a mountain;
Shower of rain in a fountain;
Figures dancing before the fires
Of their imagination.

Chas Warlow

HELP

               When night
Claps down her perforated lid,
Traps glow-worm lamps on sentry-go, the
Lions of London nod, finally fall to
Dreaming.   *Quiet*
Whispers, then, of wonders so timid, a
Cat's purr frightens them off, though
Mousemen step into their own at last, to
Hear themselves whistle,
Echoes skipping from house to house
Dozing till dawn.

              On cold nights
Trees walk wide streets to keep warm,
But in parks must huddle under the
Dread noses of owl-eyes roosting, and in
Fearful sight of policemen who would
Question their going.

Beneath the streets
Dragons rumble dungeon-chains, their breath at
Manholes (or at Women's holes) reeking poison except
Weed-flowers burst pavement-flags,
Sweeten the air.

But *light* does burn -
High at a window atop a tower - a
Last signal, all voice
Long drowned in currents of argument,
Minds gone,
Lost in a maze.

Oliver Cox

DAWNING SEA

Early each summer morning when I'm called,
I look down from the heights along the vale.
Where greying mists of dawn lie low and long,
Joining land and sky into a nebulous whole.
The clouds round off the mists for like a body palled
This amorphous shape runs through the dale.
Yet from the mist emerge some shapes so strong.
White triangles of sailing ships heading for a goal.
After the rising sun has burned away
Those all concealing mists. Hills and a farm,
Roads and trees. All of these are seen.
Simple rural life as its always been.
But now those ships of grace have lost their charm.
An eyesore now. Huge spoils of Cornish clay.

Zoe Ryle

DAL LAKE

Our small shikara gently rocks our watery path
Which mirrors single grasses growing through the lakes.
The nimble-footed water-birds, they hop from pad
To large green lily pad. Above, the dragonflies,
With laughing wings and playful tunes, dance out their dreams
And yearn to be sun in sparkling greeny-blue.
The wax-exuding lily buds glow fat and pink.
They smile upon the lake like blueful baby moons
Too eager to reflect the leafy lake-lit skies.
In lush green waterways the weeds have had no pain;
They grow as if to make their friendly world a bed
And bid us sway in sleeping cradles sweet with sun.

Rachael Noronha

ESSENCE

I express myself
best
when I dance,
that's when I feel
free.
Arabesques, contractions, jétés,
hold feelings that
excite me.

Nothing beats the heat that rises,
when my soul into volcano turns.
My flesh erupts pure hot lava,
energy from a higher world.

When I dance I am
all elements,
nothing is beyond me.
I am a raging,
destructive, meteorite
and,
gentle, twilight soliloquy.

Laura Annansingh

REJECTION

I thought that we could
be something you and I.
But now it seems as though
my thoughts ran away
with my heart, and its
time to try to calm the
fluttering beat and hide the tears
when you gently
push me away.
What have I done that
is so wrong? Made you get
in touch with what you really feel
deep down inside, all
that you want to keep hidden
never to be shown?
Don't hurt me,
I've been hurt so many times
before. Thought it was different,
this time, so different,
But no, I am the
one who ends up hurting and crying,
pretending to be
oh so brave. But
my tears are there
to be seen, my hurting is there
to be felt,
my pain is there
to be relived,
as you gently
push me away.

NAT

FAITHFUL FRIEND

Old tree burnt black and blue
Lying Kent's meadow vale
Many my worries I lay on you
Many a prayer, disaster, and tale

When your branches reached out to touch me
When your leaves caressed my brow
When your years of wisdom calmed me
Where you met perils with toil and frown

Now that your term has ended
As blocks upon a grate
I feel that my worries have extended
I am faced with utter fate
For who has time to listen
In this world of wax filled ears
Of plastic people pouting
Life's toil they could not serve.

Colin Taylor

THE MOBILE PHONE

Is there somewhere on this planet
Where I can be alone?
Far away from the latest curse,
That damn infernal, mobile phone!

The biggest mouth, the loudest voice,
Your stuck with it, you have no choice,
How can you complain or make a fuss,
When you are sitting in a crowded bus.

Yelling and shouting in the street,
As a friend in Australia they try to greet,
I've heard it said, I'm sure it's true,
They even use those damn phones in the loo.

With phone stuck to a contorted face,
The restaurant or any public place,
Private business heard by all,
When it's supposed to be a personal call!

Ron Duck

SPANCIL MY THOUGHTS FOR THEY MAY SPANCIL ME

The question is; are our thoughts our own?
I think not
For once a thought has taken root
who knows where it will end.

They may bury some of us
They may raise others to unfathomable height
They may change the course of history
or open up new horizons

They have delved to inner and outer space
They have imploded and exploded
They have sucked out of the future and
sucked out of the past and spat into the present

They have twisted and taunted us
They have given us escape and abandonment
They have freed us to dream.
Thoughts have made us kings and slaves

Who is the puppeteer of our minds?

Margaret Dunne

THE DEMISE OF BIG - BAD 'BUTCHER - BEN'

Through old London streets of fog and damp, lit by light
                                          of flickering lamp
Down quaint alleyways of cobblestone, at dead of night
                                          he walked alone
Undercover of a moonless dark, where stray cats prowl
                                          and hound-dogs bark
In Stepney, oozed rich blood of life, old 'Butcher-Ben'
                                          wiped clean his knife

Bow Street Runners, ran the City Road, in Old Street caught
                                            the 'slimy toad'!
Bruised, Ben awoke with telling scars in Newgate prison
                                        behind black bars
Dappled horses pulled the prison cart, to the criminal
                                        courts for trials start
At the dock the prisoner stood, hands cuffed and chained
                                        for public good

In the courtroom swirled tobacco smoke and livers squirmed
                                            in clarets soak
'Lord Justice Slipknott' drank his share, fine port in bottle
                                          beside his chair
The judge bewigged was looking stern, his stomach raw
                                          with ulcer-burn
From behind his bench his verdict came vociferous tongues
                                            fell quickly lame

'I find you guilty, 'more or less', though of murder foul you
                                            won't confess
You will be taken from this place, to please the gallows 'just in case'!
May God have mercy on your soul, yet your heart be black as coal'
'Well done judge, you've done us proud!' brayed the drunken
                                            courtroom crowd

Lord Justice Slipknott knew the ropes, 'Just stretch their necks,
                                                                           until they chokes!'
A crowd turned out in red contempt, for murder blue an end undreamt
'I am innocent!' came again Ben's plea, 'I didn't do it!' he cried
                                                                                 plaintively
But . . . mercy swung by hangman's rope and 'Ben' by neck,
                                                                         his collar broke!

Xerox (Psyche) Pendragon

THE STORM

We stood there in the road
watching the night time.
The sky was too heavy,
weighed down by starless black.
Our bodies tingled, charged
in the electric air.
A heavy mist hung moist
around our feet,
like hot expectant breath;
whispering the weather.
Down came the rain.
A torrent of cool water,
hammering about our heads
like icy needles.
Soaking our skin while we
held hands with the lightening.

Julieanne Jude Murphy

RAIN

It is a dance in mud
Or penetration of the roofs of temples.
Time is not measured
But by the pulse outside
Or the interior echoing stillness.
Agitator of the ages
And exhaltant of odours
It becomes rice fields
And perfumes of the past.
Flesh, flower and vegetation
Revive their spirits
Ghostlike.
Nobody counts the minutes.
All listen to the rain
Or breathe in, freely.
Some raging and some rinsing
Sound in the patter and rustling.
Old men and children
Are walking about in the rain,
Secure under their hats.
Now, bones are being washed.
The rain touches mankind.

Alasdair Aston

I AM NO LONGER

feelings of shame and guilt
surrounded my world for a time,
worry! Confusion!
In my life in my dreams,
all this, and I done nothing.

My young life wrenched from my body,
I was left in a state of lost innocence,
with a broken mind, a fearful heart
and images of misery and sadness.

From a child to a woman,
a victim to a survivor,
I am now at peace and undivided,
I have found a new spirit, a muscle security
because I have dealt with this rage that burned me.

I am no longer that frightened child
who fears for what may come,
I am a woman who once carried
the ache and the torment,
and turned it into something peaceful.

Natasha Cameron

JOBBER'S BLUES

This life imperfection is a way of life
injecting us affected with daily strife,
it's not conducive to your very good health
no feel-good here, just dreams of wealth.

From the place and duty you've grown to despise
to the sole trader struggling to survive,
labour of love seems so rare
stuck in the treadmill, a living nightmare.

No time or mood for even the simplest pleasures
the system's got your every measure.
It's a financial means to an end,
serving only to drive you round the bend.

Feeling insecure, with the fear of expulsion
life's surely too short to just merely function.
Live your dreams, have more fun, keep happy and stress-free
This isn't a dress rehearsal, so it's the best way to be.

John A Singh

THE BRIDE

Yesterday I teased and flirted,
I was promised, but not yet wed.
Today we gave each other rings,
Each to the other vows were said.
Tonight, among the silks and jewels,
Rejoicing, every dance I led.

Now I wait in virginal white,
On trembling shoulders unbound hair,
Stripped of supportive finery,
Stripped also of my savoir faire.

He approaches, throat uncovered,
Rich wedding clothes aside are laid.
I saw my brothers scantily clad,
Why does his flesh make me afraid?
I have danced and I have feasted,
But now the piper must be paid.

Eunice Patel

SHOPPING

Miriam goes shopping every day
In her local shop she goes to pay
For goods she has bought
Or so she thought
One busy afternoon
The security guard staring
Whistling a tune
Miriam cheerfully carried on
Shopping
Her uniform neatly pressed
The guard won't let Miriam rest
Till she has worn her out
Looking round without a doubt
Shopping
Not stealing like she thinks
'Don't look suspicious.'
Miriam blinks and thinks
Shopping
Such a pain, so much work
Convince them you're far from sin
Only shopping
Her friend is busy today
She makes this so much easier
No time for play or
Shopping
Miriam wants her there
For if she is, there is no fear
In shopping
No guard watching day and night
Friends relaxed, not uptight
For miriam's friend is white . . .
When she is there
No self-awareness
Just shopping.

Catherine Isichei

THE BOY

She watches, staring
Her heart warms, caring
The boy sits down
On his face, a frown
By his mouth, a flute
On his feet, one boot
He plays his tune, not missing a note
His sea of melodies with him on a boat
She's now miles away, happy and proud
But in her heart the music's still loud.

J Davies

THE DUEL

Weapons drawn, the rivals face,
each other in this crowded place.
The bright light glints on sharpened points,
and sweat each glistening brow anoints.
The sound of thudding blows are heard,
the crowd drops silent, not a word,
escapes their lips, excitement mounts,
these two are here to square accounts.
Each man a hero to the crowd,
eyes the other, heads unbowed,
as both display their awesome skill,
defeat would be a bitter pill.
Now the battle's reached its height,
as each man strives with all his might, to grasp the crown
that's won their hearts,
and yet, they're only playing darts.

James Poole

UNTITLED

At last the sun
on my face to wake me.
Something huge
is turning underground cogs
of glorious beginnings.
Swollen blue buds
are grenade quiet.
Kiss to bee and butterfly,
kiss to beech,
still wearing last year's skirt:
And brittle sweet chestnuts'
crow dotted head, waits,
waddi barked,
for a namesake
who rises earlier
with buds asticky
and heavy dishcloth leaves.
April is knocking buds from twigs,
twigs from branches.
Moss from roofs
and petals from the bloom,
cobwebs away
and water from the head.
As the trumpets fade
the bells begin.
This year's flowers
fall on last year's seed.

P Schofield

ONLY A STREET AWAY

London is full of quiet places, if you know where to go.
Small secluded spaces, cared for plants, benches to sit on,
possibilities of rest, at peace with your own thoughts, breath,

choosing to read, write, or just reflect during
a snatched lunch-break sneaked in a working day,
and traffic roar is dim, yet only a street away

'Spare some change,' 'Help the homeless,'
'Buy the big issue.' Big issues indeed.
Strange how these chants are now part of city life.

If I give to everyone, I too, might be sitting there like you,
huddled on cardboard, newspapers, sleeping in doorways, begging,
barefoot, wrapped in old decaying clothes, and blankets.

Jean Beith

HOPE

He, the height of manhood,
demanding all things good.
She a fair princess
of love and gentleness.

They learnt to live together,
in a world sometimes harsh.
Toiling with endeavour,
Their beauty fading fast.

A young family grew,
from a love strong and true.
Mid hardship none the less,
A union of success.

If life is too easy,
mankind will cease to strive.
Richness makes us lazy.
Far better to be wise.

Wendy Edwards

LONDON TRAFFIC JAM

Yesterday
I met men and horses on their way
to jazz up that absurd array,
the Earls Court Royal Tournament.
Bugles blew.
I counted horses: forty-two,
six teams and extras. Road rage grew
at this bizarre impediment.
By next year
I don't suppose they'll still be there.
Gun-carriages are getting rare
and then they're used for ornament.
All the same.
to ban the King's Troop would be visual shame:
jam's exalted when this lot's to blame:
way's blocked by golden sediment.

P S Joll

THE LAND

Waking up in the early morn
It makes me glad that I was born
Through the day I work hard on the land
And build my house with mortar and sand

To plough and sow this fertile field
So bumper crops they will yield
The morning sky so very blue
Over this land is a wonderful hue

The earth is rich, dark and mellow
Daffs are blooming, soft and yellow
I walk in the garden when there are showers
Just to smell the sweet scent of flowers

The birds are singing it's a joy to hear
I feel so alive each day of the year
To sit in moonlight by the stream
This has always been my dream

No-one will ever understand
The love I have for this here land
Part of it, will be with me
From now, until eternity.

Valerie Deering

UDDERLY COWED

Mad about the Beef
We're all mad about the Beef
With Europe declining
And Britain not signing
We're all mad about the Beef.

Oh to be finally free
Of the dreaded BSE
Plus of course the vet's guarantee
To end all present uncertainty

Now the Veggies and Vegans come into their own
Carrots and spuds aren't cut from the bone
Opportunity knocks. Gardeners please raise the tone
All produce in future organically grown.

Bryn Bartlett

YOU'VE COME OUT TO PLAY

I know you so well
Yet I've pushed you away
Contained in your shell
Now you've come out to play

Ignorantly I nurture
Your unique sides and lines
You've withstood the torture
An injury that blinds

Disappearing cushions
Left you lying flat
Pondering the questions
And then slowly you sat

Your posture corrected
You can join in the game
Your movements perfected
No longer lame.

Emma Lawrence

TARAF

Iranians have a wonderful name for an empty statement or promise.
Taraf
A very descriptive word, with absolutely no room for compromise.
Taraf
When an errant lover says, 'I love you,' and doesn't.
Taraf
When a coquette says, 'Oh, the expense - you really mustn't.'
Taraf
When a seaside postcard says, 'Wish you were here!'
Taraf
When a fatty says, 'I'll become obese if I eat this I fear.'
Taraf
When a boy writes home to his mother, 'Eating well and working hard.'
Taraf
When a poker player smiles as he studies his cards.
Taraf
'I would never get involved in *that* sort of thing.'
Taraf
'Can't stop I'm in a hurry, I'll give you a ring.'
Taraf

Linda Miller

INFORMATION

We hope you have enjoyed reading this book - and that you will continue to enjoy it in the coming years.

If you like reading and writing poetry drop us a line, or give us a call, and we'll send you a free information pack.

Write to :-
**Anchor Books Information
1-2 Wainman Road
Woodston
Peterborough
PE2 7BU
(01733) 230761**